Islands of Wonder
HAWAI'I
THE BIG ISLAND

Photography by
Douglas Peebles

Library of Congress Control Number: 2013952301
ISBN-13: 978-1939487-26-1
First Printing, January 2014

Mutual Publishing, LLC
1215 Center Street, Suite 210
Honolulu, Hawai'i 96816
Ph: 808-732-1709 / Fax: 808-734-4094
email: info@mutualpublishing.com
www.mutualpublishing.com

Printed in Korea

INTRODUCTION

Hawai'i has been called a melting pot, a term often used to represent the blend of ethnic groups that have settled here. But the Island of Hawai'i blends far more than ethnicities. It is a crucible where the formative forces of the volcano meet the destructive powers of erosion, a place where the high-tech world of modern astronomy rubs shoulders with cattle ranching and flower farming, and where microclimates have blossomed into a diverse and unique natural environment. In this melting pot, the array of ethnicities is just another player.

A million-and-a-half visitors each year arrive to join in the mix. They trek to active volcanoes and hear legends about how ancient deities transformed these landscapes. They visit lush jungles and tropical beaches where protected sea turtles haul out. They cruise through old Hawaiian cattle ranches peppered with modern windmills. They park in restored plantation towns where food, art and shopping have replaced the once-dominant sugar industry. They savor fresh fish dishes with a view of the ocean and check out the coffee and macadamia nut farms. They hike through national parks, botanic gardens, and restored archaeological sites.

The many nationalities brought to the Islands to work the sugar fields are an important part of the Hawaiian melting pot. To visit the island is to be immersed in the diversity of its coastal vistas, its quiet bays and rugged cliffs, its bustling villages and its misty uplands, its icy peaks with telescopes trained on the distant stars. But also its people, in all their own diversity.

Punalu'u Black Sand Beach, a picturesque stretch of sand built by old lava flows, is what visitors anticipate seeing when they visit the island of Hawai'i. Add the region's tall, swaying palm trees, coconuts and honu, or Hawaiian green sea turtles, and it doesn't get any better. Punalu'u also offers a freshwater pond with ducks and wading areas full of chilly water directly from natural springs.

Preceding page: The eeriness of Halema'uma'u Crater never fails to send a shiver up one's spine as steam and gases rise from the depths and blinding, flickering colors dance along the rim and into the air. Halema'uma'u is an opportunity to catch a glimpse of what's boiling beneath the surface of Kilauea.

Hilo has maintained its small town friendliness and relaxed lifestyle. A walk through downtown Hilo leads past wooden-front Japanese and Chinese stores to simple stone structures transformed into modern cafes. Reed's Bay, described in the last century as "a picturesque inlet, with residences along its shores," is the largest natural bay along Hilo's shoreline and has become a popular boating harbor. On the Waiākea peninsula (center), the famous Banyan Drive leads visitors to Hilo's largest hotels with the Naniloa Volcanoes Resort on the point. On the western edge is the beautifully landscaped Japanese-style Lili'uokalani Gardens with a footbridge to Coconut Island.

HILO

Peaceful, old Hilo has the charm of a South Pacific town. Rivers run through it. Frame buildings along its waterfront have overlooked its streets for generations. A rich volcanic soil and heavy rainfall ensure that with few exceptions, if it can grow, it will grow in and around Hilo. The town's daily farmer's market celebrates that food and flower productivity.

Hilo was once one of the main ports in Hawai'i. Later, it served the sugar industry, as it lay central between the great sugar regions of Hāmākua and Puna. As sugar production declined, Hilo became a service town, with headquarter offices for the astronomical observatories atop Mauna Kea, a four-year college and the seat of county government. Hilo has an active shipping port and in international airport, and it remains a jumping-off point for trips to Kīlauea Volcano and Hawai'i Volcanoes National Park.

In many ways, Hilo is a town for Hawai'i's residents more than for its visitors. It is less sun and surf, and more land and culture. The Hawaiian heritage is everywhere. Most communities have a single outrigger canoe club; Hilo has several, and hundreds of paddlers work out on Hilo Bay each day.

The active astronomy program atop Mauna Kea is celebrated at Hilo's 'Imiloa Astronomy Center, which is funded by several of the big telescope outfits. Lyman Museum shares the island's history. The Pacific Tsunami Museum and Mokupāpapa Discovery Center provide information about things closer to sea level. For quiet reflection, Hilo has Lili'uokalani Gardens and Coconut Island.

Hilo is so full of diversity that it is hard to pigeonhole.

Above: Leleiwi Beach Park in Hilo offers great scenery and opportunities to enjoy the best aspects of Hawai'i. The beaches and coves are home to a variety of sea life, from wildly colored reef fish to sea turtles and dolphins. Whether picnicking, meandering through the parks and lagoons, or boogie boarding, note that these recreation areas can fill up fast on holidays and weekends.

Left: Beehive gingers are among more than 2,000 varieties of flowers and other plants at Hilo's Hawai'i Tropical Botanical Garden. This preserve sits on 40 acres and has its own greenhouse set amid cascading waterfalls, gurgling streams and scenic viewpoints.

Opposite page: Cascading 442 feet through a tropical rain forest of giant ginger, heliconia, ferns, orchids, and bamboo, 'Akaka Falls is one of Hawai'i's tallest waterfalls. This riveting cascade of water plummets into a gorge eroded by streams. Abundant mists rise from the falls, which are located within 63-acre 'Akaka Falls State Park, approximately four miles southwest of Honomū.

In the morning, when the sun is just right, rainbows shimmering in the misty spray of the aptly named Rainbow Falls, located above downtown Hilo, seem to drop into a deep, dark pool. Hilo's famed rainfall, approximately 133 inches a year, explains the plentiful waterfalls. Water descending from the mountains irrigated the ancient Hawaiian taro cultivation systems. So essential was water to the well-being of a village that the Hawaiian word for wealth is "waiwai," meaning abundant water.

Left: A lone man stands and watches an outrigger canoe on the sands of Hilo Bayfront Park. A cultural tradition rooted in early Hawaiian history, canoe paddling has become a favorite team sport for all islanders, revived in places such as Hilo Bay, which hosts major paddling events. Skilled woodworkers, themselves often paddlers with intimate knowledge of the ocean, craft many of the paddles. Koa was a favored wood in years past, although some paddles are now made with synthetic materials, metals and lighter woods.

Right: Kamehameha Street is home to a variety of bustling shops, galleries, and restaurants. Some artisans here create Hawaiian bowls or weave lauhala mats. Kamehameha Street embodies the tempo of life and hospitality that is associated with Hilo and Hawai'i Island.

Left: The Hilo Farmers Market is one of the top places to find anything and everything local from the island. From its humble beginnings in 1988, when a handful of farmers sold produce from the backs of their trucks, the market now boasts more than 200 vendors with products ranging from the freshest fruits and vegetables to ornate tropical flowers, crafts and goods that are ideal gifts. This award-winning market continues to grow and even has information available online, yet it retains its down-to-earth charm.

Right: Traditionally, anthuriums were red and heart-shaped, but breeders have taken their flowers into new territory with different shapes, colors and sizes. Originally from tropical America, these flowers now grow wild in many shaded Big Island valleys. Greenhouse-grown blooms are an important island industry. Fresh bunches of anthuriums are ready for sale at the Hilo open market.

Snow-capped Mauna Kea (foreground) and Mauna Loa (looming in the distance) are Hawai'i's two most massive volcanic mountains. The snow goddess Poli'ahu resided on Mauna Kea's frozen summit during her many battles with the fire goddess Pele. Since the installation of a first observatory on the mountain in 1970, the 13,796-foot Mauna Kea has emerged as the world's leading astronomical site. It is home to thirteen telescope facilities staffed by astronomers from eleven countries, including the Keck Observatory Center.

Waipi'o Valley, isolated by imposing cliffs and a rough, white-capped bay, is one of the last vestiges of a Hawai'i tied to the 'āina, or land. Its taro farmers pursue their livelihoods much as their predecessors did when the valley was the home of the island's highest-ranking Hawaiian chiefs including Liloa, 'Umi, and the legendary Kamehameha. Some farmers live in the valley; others live on the ridge above and use 4-wheel-drive vehicles on the steep, zig-zag road to the valley floor. Sparsely populated today, it's hard to believe that Waipi'o was home to an estimated 4,000 residents at the time of the European

HĀMĀKUA

The lush Hāmākua coastline north of Hilo forms the windward shoulder of Mauna Kea and collects impressive amounts of tradewind rain. That rainfall has eroded away the land to form Hāmākua's jagged valleys, but also irrigates the rich farming plateaus between them.

Sugar cane was once the dominant crop here, but today the old cane fields grow timber, macadamia nut, papaya, mango and many more exotic crops. A train museum recalls the days when locomotives hauled sugar cane and people up and down the coast. Many of the old sugar plantation towns celebrate the handiwork of the children of sugar workers, and you will find historic buildings full of handicrafts, woodwork, art and history.

Towering highway bridges span the gorges, and quiet roads twist down to the few accessible shores. One of the first little towns north of Hilo is quaint Honomū, the gateway to famed ʻAkaka Falls.

At Laupāhoehoe, a small park and a memorial commemorate the tsunami that wiped out much of a generation of this coastal plateau. It happened on April Fool's Day, 1946, and the community has never recovered.

Among the most active villages is Honokaʻa, once the headquarters of the Hāmākua Sugar Company, and now a restored historic community celebrated for its art and music, including the Hāmākua Music Festival, which is held each fall.

Hāmākua's coastline is bracketed by Hilo to the south and Waipiʻo to the north. Waipiʻo, viewed from a high scenic overlook, still looks much as it must have when Captain Cook arrived here, checkerboarded with taro fields and rich in undeveloped scenic splendor.

Above: The fingers of chilly water, cutting for tens of thousands of years through the Hāmākua Coast lava, formed rugged features such as Maulua ("difficult") Bay. In the years before bridges, Isabella Bird and other Victorian visitors traversing these gulches were lifted by rope up and down the sheer precipices.

Left: Wild horses are found throughout Waipiʻo Valley and along the Hāmākua Coast. Originally brought in to help the taro farmers, these magnificent animals know no boundaries and are now considered to be more of a nuisance to those growers remaining in the area. It is still an exciting moment when they can be seen.

Opposite page: Waipiʻo Valley has lush greenery, an abundance of rain, and entrances with breathtaking scenery. The "Land of Curving Water" stretches several miles along the northern tip of the island of Hawaiʻi between Hāmākua and Kohala, and was the home of Hawaiian kings and gods. Some of the most sacred and significant heiau on the island were located in this valley, including Pakaʻalana, a temple and place of refuge.

Left: Mauna Kea graces the skyline above an empty road in upper Hāmākua that links once-bustling sugar towns. At one time, sugar cane fields stretched up and down the coast, covering every available acre of land. Following the 1993 closing of the last remaining mill operated by Hāmākua Sugar Company, the landscape is now no longer commanded by green cane fields or obscured by the smoke that darkened the skies when cane was burned prior to harvest.

Below: Laupāhoehoe Bay was hit hard by the 1946 tsunami that destroyed most of downtown Hilo. Much of the low-lying peninsula was swept over by the wave, including an elementary school built close to the waterfront. Four teachers and twenty students were killed. The tsunami marked the demise of a once-bustling settlement, which had an active business using small boats to haul passengers and cargo to ships anchored offshore.

Opposite page, top: The wide, firm sand of the beach at Waipiʻo, with its backdrop of stark green cliffs, provides a scenic spot for a horseback ride.
Bottom: Laupāhoehoe is a flat, lava peninsula that juts out into the ocean from the Hāmākua Coast. Primarily a fishing spot today, the peninsula was formed by a flow from the now-dormant Mauna Kea, which looms over the coast. Laupāhoehoe can be reached by a steep, switchback road leading down from the uplands.

During heavy rain, waterfalls form in every groove on the near-vertical face of Waimanu Valley. Using a trail that starts to the north of Waipiʻo Valley, daring travelers enter remote, generally unpopulated Waimanu, Honopue, Honokeʻā, Honokāne Iki, and Honokāne Nui valleys, leading finally to Pololū. As late as the nineteenth century, Hawaiian villages could be found in each, but isolation and the discovery of alternative life styles depopulated the area. Today seabirds, along with a handful of hikers, hunters, archaeologists and refugees from civilization, find sanctuary on this stark coastline.

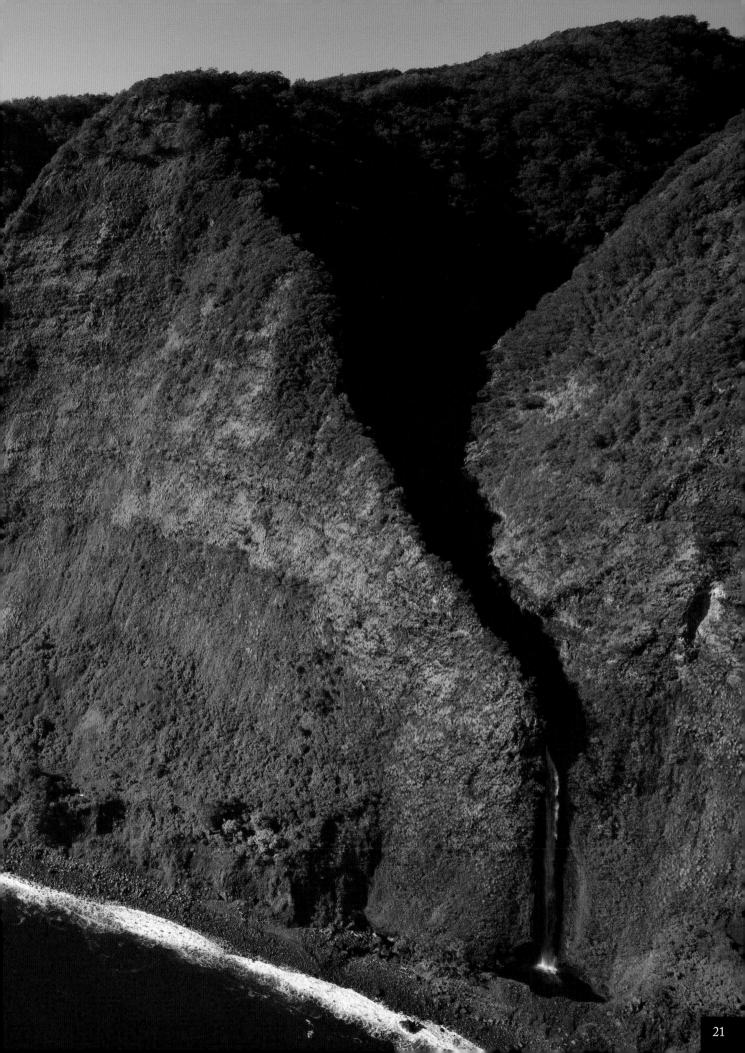

Powerful waves smash against lava flowing into the sea from Kīlauea, which has been continuously active since 1983. The battle between the land and sea goes back and forth, altering the island's landscape and constantly reshaping its coastline. Lava temperatures may reach 2,000 degrees. In legend, when fire goddess Pele bathes in the sea, the ocean boils. Lava quick-hardens and shatters as it hits the sea, and tiny grains of volcanic glass accumu-

VOLCANO

Hawai'i Island is defined by its volcanic origin in ways few other islands can match. The active volcano Kīlauea has been spewing lava for more than two decades, building new land at the coastline and covering with molten rock much of what grew or was built here.

On this island, in an afternoon, you can visit hot Kīlauea rock that's just minutes old, or at Kohala, weathered rock that's a million years old. But it's not all fire and barren landscapes in volcano land. Flourishing native forests and roads lined with fruit trees are also common, as are beaches with sand of many colors.

The rocky districts of the island, in Hawaiian mythology, belonged to the fire goddess, Pele. In legend, as in reality, the volcano constantly confronts the vegetated parts of the island, as lava flows smoke their way through stands of native forest. Hawaiian legend says this represents the pitched battle between fiery Pele and her male rival, Kamapua'a.

Visitors to Hawai'i Volcanoes National Park can view up close the legacy of live volcanoes at an informative visitors center, but also along trails to great beds of lava, by steaming vents and through volcanic tubes. Despite the active volcanism, much of the park remains native forest, which the park service actively manages.

Far to the south, at windy Ka Lae, windmills swing their arms like ancient giants. On the coast, the waves eroding an olivine-rich cinder cone create a natural wonder—a green sand beach. Offshore at South Point, opposing currents wrapping around the island meet to create a rich fishing ground in deep water near the shore.

Kīlauea is among the most active volcanoes in the world. Its lava fountain feeds a river of orange-red molten rock. The spectacular lava fountains of Puʻu ʻŌʻō cinder cone take many shapes, and some see images of Pele—sometimes as a woman in a long red muʻumuʻu. In its first three and a half years, Puʻu ʻŌʻō erupted 47 times, creating a cone 830 feet high with a pit 1,000 feet across. The volcanic action sometimes changes location, but it continues to the pres-

A lava flow travels miles down the mountainside, sometimes on the surface and sometimes enclosed in lava tubes, before finally reaching the sea. This coastline can be treacherous for bystanders intent on getting close to the action. The foundation is fragile and can sag and shift. Lava tubes can collapse, and a severed tube can gush a fire hose of incandescent lava for many hours.

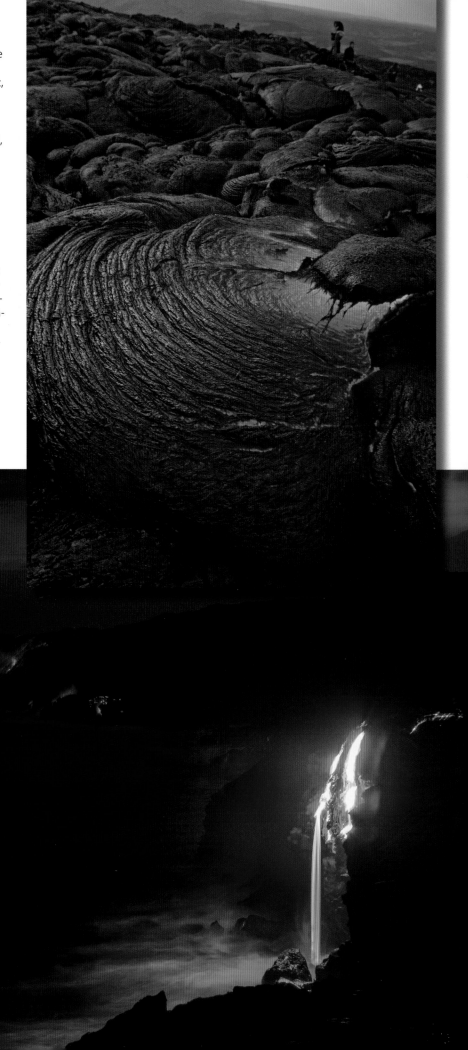

Right: Hiking on new pāhoehoe lava gives one an up-close view of its rippling, shiny surface. Pāhoehoe lava is different from its counterpart, 'a'ā lava, because it travels more slowly and folds and ripples smoothly, which is why the word was later adopted for by Hawaiians to also describe satin. 'A'ā lava, on the other hand, advances quickly despite appearing more solid—the interior is actually still fluid. Trails maintained by the National Park Service take visitors to a range of volcanic features. When conditions are right, explorers can hike to the place where steaming, glowing lava hits the sea.

Below: Few sights are more breathtaking than a nighttime encounter of molten lava with the cool Pacific Ocean. The sea is said to be the domain of Namakaokaha'i, Pele's jealous and temperamental sister, and the meeting between the lava and water reflects their relationship—ranging from tender to tempestuous.

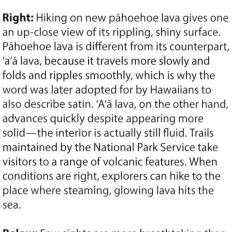

Above: The entry to the Thurston Lava Tube offers an opportunity to walk inside a natural tunnel where lava once flowed. This cool, subterranean tunnel in the midst of jungle ferns is an estimated 400 years old and gives explorers a dramatic picture of the dramatic forces that continue to shape the island of Hawai'i.

Left: A vent in the Halema'uma'u Crater contains a lake of fire that restlessly bubbles and swirls. The crater has seen continuous activity since its eruption in 2008. No safe viewing areas are close enough to see the actual lake, but its glow is easily visible from park overlooks at night.

Above: This native ʻōhiʻa tree is a striking portrait against the stark landscape found at the bottom of Kīlauea Iki, a small crater just outside Kīlauea Crater near the Thurston Lava Tube. Starting in the rain forest, a trail leads from the upper rim to the steaming crater floor, where very little else is found among its desolation besides the ʻōhiʻa trees that have sprung up out of the lava to dominate the scenery.

Left: The kahili ginger, a relative of edible ginger, is one of an array of exotic, fragrant blooms growing wild on the island. Ranging from four to eight feet in height, this plant is an invasive species whose dense roots choke out native vegetation in moist forest areas.

Opposite page, top: Rain forests are complex ecosystems. These tall ʻōhiʻa trees protect a range of ferns, vines, and shrubs growing below. Native ʻamaʻu ferns, whose young fronds have a reddish tint, are native only to the Hawaiian Islands and can be found in Volcanoes National Park as well as around the island. **Bottom:** Kīlauea's lavas destroyed parts of Puna even as they helped built new land. In 1990, lava flowed through the old fishing town of Kalapana and helped create the famous black-sand beach of Kaimū. These new beaches are among the youngest landforms of the Earth.

Tree ferns shade the forest floor under an open canopy of primarily ʻōhiʻa trees within Hawaiʻi Volcanoes National Park. ʻŌhiʻa have a unique growth form that has both ground and aerial roots. The trees are among the first plants to spring up in new lava fields.

Above: The Pahoa-Pohoiki Road is also known as Mango Grove Road. The massive fruit trees line its narrow paved lanes and form a tunnel of branches and foliage. This twisting thoroughfare leads through much of Puna and its small farms and towns.

Opposite page: Gnarly natural sculptures in Lava Tree State Park, off Highway 132, are silent witnesses to Mauna Loa's power. In 1790, its molten lava hit Puna's rain forest, hardening around the 'ōhi'a trees to form basalt molds. While the trees themselves quickly died, the tree molds remained.

Right: Mitsubishi wind generators at South Point's windmill farm stand stark amid the pastures. This farm is one of several on the island. The wind blows almost constantly here, and the windmills fill the air with an eerie sound. Wind and geothermal power are major sources of renewable energy on Hawai'i Island.

Below: Ka Lae, also known as South Point, is the southernmost spot in the United States. According to one legend, it is where the first human beings settled in the Hawaiian Islands. The area has extensive archaeological re- mains, like these carved canoe mooring rocks near the Kalalea fishing shrine. The Big Island has beaches in many colors. The green sand beach near Ka Lae. Black sand is from fresh lava hitting the ocean or eroded volcanic rock, while Hawaiian white sand is finely crushed shell, coralline algae and bits of other aquatic life. The elusive red-sand beaches come from the erosion of a cinder cone. Green sand is the result of olivine crystals in the lava.

Above: This rare hawksbill turtle at Puna's Punalu'u Black Sand Beach enjoys the shallow reefs and cold spring-fed oceanic waters. Protected species like green sea turtles and the hawksbills are often spotted here. Punalu'u Beach Park is one of the most accessible black-sand beaches on the island and its coconut groves, ponds and exposed reefs make it a favorite spot.

Left: These black-sand beaches along the lush Puna coast are among the newest lands of Earth. Lava is constantly reshaping the shoreline. An ancient chant, "Pau Puna, ua ko'ele ka papa" translates to, "Puna is ravaged; the foundation crackles."

The green sand beach at Ka Lae, sometimes called Mahana Beach and sometimes Papakōlea, is renowned. Its unique olivine crystal sand actually sparkles. The olivine has been deposited by surf that beats on the base of Pu'u Mahana, a volcanic cone whose lava is rich in the semi-precious green stone. The cone is sometimes called Pu'u O Mahana.

KONA

Kona brings to mind the rich aroma of good coffee, the smell of the ocean, the tang in the air from the volcanic eruption over the mountain, and the waft of fresh catch for dinner from the many restaurants on the shorefront.

It is renowned for its tourism attributes, not the least of which is sun nearly every day. Rain is rare. It's on the leeward side, so the ocean is normally calm. The water is a clear blue.

Kona is the island's playland. Outrigger canoes ply the offshore waters. Charter fishing boats, heading out with the dawn, chase after the tuna and marlin for which these waters are famous. Surfers ride a few reef breaks when a swell from the west rises up. Snorkelers find wonders throughout the coastline on the coral-crusted lava.

There are hotels in town, but the famed resorts of North Kona and South Kohala string out to the left of town, as you face inland. These are oases carved out of the arid lava lands, luxurious hotels on rare sandy beaches and championship golf courses among the vast slabs of black stone. Areas that may not be best for swimming are incredible spots for snorkeling, surfing and kayaking.

To the south are the sites of Captain James Cook's death at Kealakekua Bay, the historic Hawaiian place of refuge, Puʻuhonua O Hōnaunau National Historical Park, and classic coffee towns like Captain Cook. Famed Kona coffee is dominated by small family farms, and you can often pick up some of the best coffee in the world in little shops by the roadside.

Mahaiʻula Beach not only has swaying palms, teal waters and inviting stretches of sand, but in the evenings it offers a front-row seat to dazzling sunsets. The smoldering orange colors so vividly seen along this part of the island are sometimes deepened by the presence of vog, the volcanic haze that drifts over from Kīlauea Volcano.

Above: Along the North Kona coast, deserted beaches await the adventuresome. Inaccessible except on foot or by canoe, secret bays such as Keawaiki Bay, with its black sand beaches, are reminders that this wild, rugged part of West Hawaiʻi has not been totally tamed.

Opposite page: Kailua Bay and Ōneo Bay at the foot of the Hualālai Volcano were the setting for historic Kailua village. Kamehameha the Great spent his last days here. Once a sleepy fishing village, Kailua-Kona today is the island's fastest growing community and a major visitor destination. Kailua preserves its history with places like the Mokuaikaua Church, the oldest surviving Christian church in the islands, built in 1837.

This sweeping panorama captures the splendor of the Keauhou Coast of Kona with its ocean blue waters, beach coves, surf sites, and boat harbors. Hualālai Mountain looms in the background. The Sheraton Kona Resort and Spa at Keauhou Bay is at the bottom right while in the middle the orange roofs of the Kona Coast Resort can be seen.

Right: Delightful Mahai'ula Beach, in Kona's Kekaha Kai State Park, takes a little work to get to because of its rugged road, but the effort is rewarded. Its salt-and-pepper sand runs into blue-green waters. The water is shallow and calm enough for snorkeling and swimming in summer with surfing taking precedence during the waves of winter.

Below: Magic Sands Beach, located along Ali'i Drive south of downtown Kailua-Kona, is also known as White Sands Beach Park. This small cove is popular for snorkeling and body boarding. When high surf rolls in, the sand drifts offshore giving the beach its third name, Disappearing Sands.

Nohea Point, in Kailua-Kona, popular for weddings and sunbathing, is a pristine nook. Thatched umbrellas and beach chairs, crystal-clear waters lapping at the stone wall that surrounds the point, and the luscious flowers and shrubs that encompass the grounds, all add to the tropical getaway feel of this retreat.

Long and sandy Mahaiʻula Beach is the perfect balance of sun and shade. Plentiful trees line up along the steep beach, providing respite from the day's heat. Cool waters invite lounging on its sands. Shallow water near shore gets deep quickly, requiring caution. Mahaiʻula Beach has the feel of a deserted island paradise.

Crescent-shaped and packed with white sand, Manini'ōwali Beach along Kua Bay is ideal for fun in the surf and sunbathing, but there is little shade. The beach, easily accessible and very popular, is a part of Kekaha Kai State Park which is primarily made up of fields of lava.

Right: Downtown Kailua-Kona, an eclectic mix of shops and beach attractions, entices tourists, honeymooners, fishing competitors, and hardcore athletes from around the world. It is home to the famous Ironman Triathlon and has a large sport fishing fleet. Kailua-Kona is one of the most active seaside towns in the Hawaiian Islands.

Below: Big-game fishing is one of Kona's trademark tourist attractions. Each August, hundreds of anglers flock here for the Hawaiian International Billfish Tournament. The rest of the year, fishing enthusiasts go not only for the billfish, but for mahimahi, ono, tuna and other marine game species.

Above: A lei vendor displays his aromatic bounty at a booth in Kailua-Kona. Lei-making is an art cherished in the Hawaiian culture. Garlands like these welcome or say farewell to loved ones, express thanks, adorn brides and birthday celebrants, or simply show appreciation.

Left: Overlooking Kahalu'u Bay, Ke'ekū Heiau stands adjacent to Hāpaiali'i Heiau. This is believed to be the site where, in the 1500s, the chief of Maui, Kamalalawalu, was sacrificed after invading and being defeated by Chief Lonoikamakahiki. These heiau have recently been restored as a reminder of Kona's complex history.

Left and below: Outrigger canoes like these at Kamakahonu Beach are a familiar sight in Kailua-Kona waters. Kailua Bay's calm seas host the world's largest long-distance outrigger events, the Queen Lili'uokalani Canoe Races. The Labor Day weekend events draw more than 2,500 paddlers and spectators.

Oppsosite page: Hulihe'e Palace, a two-story stone mansion in the Western style, was built on the Kailua-Kona seafront by Governor Kuakini in 1837 and 1838. It was the Kona residence of royal governors and the kings and queens of Hawai'i whenever they visited the coast. It was not popular with Princess Ruth "Luka" Ke'elikōlani, the Hawai'i Island governor from 1855 to 1869. She chose to live in a native grass house in Hilo. Today, the palace has reopened as a museum and hula dancers often gather to practice and perform on its oceanfront grounds.

In about 1650, Chief Keawe constructed this thatched house to store the bones of dead ali'i (chiefs) at Pu'uhonua O Hōnaunau, now a national historical park. The chief, originally from Kona, also united the island's eastern Hilo and western Kona districts.

Originally built in the 1500s, Pu'uhonua O Honaunau, an ancient "place of refuge," was one of the most sacred areas on the island. It was the largest of 10 pu'uhonua on the island and was protected by a massive L-shaped wall. Once 1,000 feet long, 10 feet high and 17 feet wide, the wall still stands today. Here, violators of the kapu laws sought sanctuary and purification, enemy warriors found safe haven, and the weak could find protection during war. Two heiau and a royal residence were also found here. The site is preserved and interpreted today by the U.S. National Park Service.

Top: Ho'okena was a busy town and boat landing during the 1800s, but the gray coral and lava-rock sands are now a tranquil beach retreat. Camping is a popular pastime for both locals and visitors, and the cliffs are famous as nesting areas for seabirds.

Bottom: Kona coffee, made from the seeds inside red coffee cherries, is arguably the best coffee in the world. It grows in a narrow strip on the upland slopes of Hualālai and Mauna Kea volcanoes, where its acreage is limited and it faces significant challenges, among them a new pest, the coffee cherry borer. Kona coffee is so expensive that it is often blended with lower-cost beans, but a coffee aficionado must at least try 100 percent Kona—it is worth the price.

Along the shore at Ka'awaloa, on Kealakekua Bay, a small pier and a white monument erected in 1874 to the memory of Captain James Cook are clearly visible. The British circumnavigator was killed on February 14, 1779, during a confrontation that followed the theft of a British ship's boat.

KOHALA

The Kohala district feels different from the rest of the island. The resort areas of South Kohala are a blend of old Hawaiian and modern luxury tourism, with little agriculture or immigration mixed in—those features so much a part of the balance of Hawai'i Island. That's because access was limited to boats and foot trails until a highway was pushed through just half a century ago. South Kohala continues to be vast stretches of rock punctuated with some of the finest resorts and golf courses known.

North Kohala also has a strong Hawaiian cultural flavor—King Kamehameha was born here; and significant sites include his birthplace, the Mo'okini Heiau and Lapakahi State Historical Park. But sugar and ranching played a large role throughout the 1800s and early 1900s, and their imprint plays large through the present day. Small towns in the Kohala Mountains are quiet, rustic and best known for their art shops and cafes.

While South Kohala is dominated by comparatively new lava, North Kohala was built from a volcano that was active a million years ago. Its soils are deep; its valleys deeply eroded. If you drive as far as the North Kohala road takes you, you reach the overlook for Pololū Valley, the beginning of rugged trail that ends at Waipi'o Valley on the Hāmākua Coast.

In upland Waimea, Hawaiian paniolo, or cowboys, still roam the range. The legacy of famed Parker Ranch is celebrated in museums and tours that showcase everything from amazing art collections to the days of the rough-and-tumble cowboys. Waimea houses the headquarters for the Canada-France-Hawai'i telescope and the twin Keck telescopes, whose observatories are atop Mauna Kea.

Mauna Kea Beach Hotel overlooks the crescent-shaped Kauna'oa Beach in Kohala, one of the region's finest bays. The white sand beach has excellent snorkeling. Mauna Loa, whose summit is often capped with snow in winter, looms in the background.

The Hilton Waikoloa Village is a fantasyland of lagoons with playful porpoises, waterways, water sports facilities, health spas, and secluded guest hideaways. With eight tennis courts and 18 holes of golf, the resort offers endless opportunities for recreation and celebration.

The centerpiece of the Mauna Lani resort is the 18-hole Francis ʻIʻi Brown championship golf course. The front nine holes are on rugged ʻaʻā lava and the back nine on smoother pāhoehoe. Together, they form something that is as much an outdoor art display as it is a golf course.

The Kohala Coast's first luxury hotel was Laurance Rockefeller's Mauna Kea Beach Resort, which opened in 1965 on land leased from Parker Ranch. It sits on the smooth white crescent of Kauna'oa Beach, one of the island's most beautiful beaches regularly visited by green sea turtles. No longer a Rockefeller property, the Mauna Kea Beach Hotel, as it is now known, boasts a world-recognized collection that includes more than 1,600 pieces of Asian and Pacific art and a golf course designed by Robert Trent Jones, Sr.

Above: Kohala's Hāpuna Beach is home to resorts like the 350-room Hāpuna Beach Prince Hotel, which was erected on a site with underground springs that bubble to the surface during heavy rainfall creating natural artesian fountains—thus the name hāpuna or "spring of life." The white-sand beach, featuring ideal conditions for boogie boarding, swimming, sunbathing and snorkeling, has consistently been rated on international Top Ten lists of best beaches.

Right: With its wonderful white sand beaches (Mauna Kea or Kauna'oa Beach shown here), it's no surprise that Kohala's coast is such a popular destination. Resorts such as the Mauna Kea Beach Hotel and Mauna Lani Resort offer premium amenities and services, while the beaches of the Gold Coast alone draw people from around the island and the world who appreciate their pristine beauty.

Opposite page: Jagged lava creates calm bays and quiet inlets, seen here in a sunset scene at Mauna Lani Resort's Makaīwa Bay. The bay is home to a beautiful fishpond as well. The small sand beach, with its secluded, crystal waters ringed with massive lava rocks, offer excellent snorkeling and swimming for those in search of serenity.

Less than a quarter century ago, Waimea was a ranching village of 2,000 people bothered more by stray cattle in the streets than by traffic. Today it is a bustling town of 10,000 with a new million-dollar Keck Observatory Center, an expanded Parker Ranch House tour, and traffic lights. The Parker Ranch Rodeo, with its riding and roping contests, takes place each year on July 4 in honor of the area's paniolo heritage.

Above: Parker Ranch is the largest privately owned cattle spread in the United States. Founded by John Palmer Parker in 1847, the 225,000-acre ranch passed through five generations to the late Richard Smart. The ranch is now held by The Parker Ranch Foundation Trust, for beneficiaries in Waimea. His 1862 Hawaiian Victorian home, Pu'u'ōpelu, with a world-class collection of impressionist art, is open to the public.

Left: Ke Ola Mau Loa Church in Waimea, also known as "The Green Church," is easy to spot with its colorful exterior. The small churches found throughout this part of the island are reminiscent of the island's rich history with its varied religious and ethnic roots.

Left: Every year on June 11, residents honor King Kamehameha with a ceremony at his statue, a parade, a music festival and a celebration full of authentic dress and ceremonial decorum. Although Kamehameha Day is acknowledged throughout the state, it is special to the people of the northern part of the Big Island, as this is the birthplace of the chief who united the islands and became its first king.

Below: Horseback riding through rolling green mountains is a common sight in Kohala. The uplands of Waimea are the heart of Hawai'i's paniolo, or cowboy, country. Grazing cattle and horses, log cabins with columns of smoke twisting from their chimneys, and Stetson hats may seem out of place in a tropical setting, but this is everyday life in this part of the island.

Above: Many of the charming ranch houses in the hills of Kohala, like this one, are now museums, art shops or information centers. The Parker Ranch Historic Homes and Gardens, the Parker Ranch Visitors Center and Museum, and the Anna Ranch Heritage Center in particular offer a greater understanding of the island's paniolo and ranching heritage.

Opposite page: On a barren Kohala slope, the windmills harness the famous and powerful winds that blow through this northwestern corner of the island. Some of the energy is used to pump water to the new coastal resorts. Their massive scale is not apparent until they are viewed from nearby.

Above: At the end of Highway 270 in windward Kohala, Pololū Valley opens to the cliff and valley coastline of this oldest part of the island. This region has been heavily eroded by weather and waves. A black-sand beach, horses grazing along the hillsides and rocky offshore islets are part of the dramatic vista.

Opposite page: Multiple waterfalls cascade into remote upper Waimanu Valley in the inaccessible areas of the northern Hāmākua and Kohala districts. The waterfalls, springs and deep, cold pools of the Kohala Mountains were important sources of irrigation water for the early taro farmers and later, the sugar plantations. The 1906 Kohala Ditch, a twenty-two-mile tunnel and open waterway system, carried upland water down to coastal sugar plantations. Some 600 Japanese workers labored for more than year to build the ditch and its tunnels. Today, the waterway serves not only farmers, but ranchers and resorts.

Above: A traditional pā'ū parade in Kohala's Hawī is held in honor of Kamehameha, following the draping of lei on his statue. Flowers and colors worn by the horses and riders represent each of the Hawaiian Islands, honoring in pageantry the king who was born near here.

Opposite page: Music, crafts, foods and smiles abound at the Saturday Honoka'a farmers market, in the Old Botelho Building downtown. The market is open year-round each Saturday for visitors and residents of nearby ranching communities. It features locally grown produce and other island specialties.

On May 1, 1883, an eight-and-a-half-foot bronze statue of Kamehameha the Great was unveiled in Kapaʻau, near his birthplace. The statue, representing Kamehameha at forty-five years of age, had been commissioned by the Hawaiian Kingdom's legislature five years earlier, to beautify Honolulu, not Kohala. But the ship carrying the nine-ton statue from Italy, where the sculptor lived, sank off the Falkland Islands. The Legislature ordered a replica, but meanwhile the original statue, suffering only minor damage, was salvaged. A ship's captain purchased the recovered statue and sold it to King Kalākaua for a handsome profit. The replacement arrived while the original was being repaired. Hawaiʻi Island's governor, Princess Kekaulike, suggested that the repaired original go to Kohala and the pristine replica remain in Honolulu.

Above: Members of the Queen Kaʻahumanu Society play an active role in the festivities surrounding Kamehameha Day in Hāwī, as do other civic organizations. Among their duties is weaving the countless lei needed to celebrate the king's day.

Below: Kiʻi pōhaku, which are old Hawaiian rock pictographs or petroglyphs, are often found carved into smooth pāhoehoe lava along well-traveled trails. The Hawaiian culture had no traditional form of writing, as Western culture knows it, but may have used petroglyphs as a means of communication. There are many classes of petroglyph imagery, some purely geometric and others representations of people, animals and common objects.

In the twelfth century, the voyager priest Pā'ao ordered the walls of Mo'okini Heiau, to be raised as high as thirty feet. In a single night, thousands of basalt stones were passed along a human chain stretching twelve miles from Pololū Valley to the temple site. Mo'okini Heiau today is under stewardship of kahu Leimomi Mo'okini Lum. The birthplace of King Kamehameha is a short distance away.

The scenic Kohala Mountain Road, Highway 250, meanders through miles of ranch land, including the 22,000-acre Kahuā Ranch, to connect the North Kohala peninsula to the town of Waimea. Kahuā is among the most advanced ranches in the state, using state-of-the-art windmill technology to both pump water and make electricity to supplement cattle ranching income.

Mo'okini Heiau   Kamehameha Statue
Hāwī   **Kapa'au**

Lapahaki State
Historical Park
Pololū Valley
KOHALA   *Waipi'o Valley*   **Honoka'a**
Kohala Mountains   **Pa'auilo**
Kawaihae   **Waimea**
Pu'ukoholā Heiau   **Laupāhoehoe**
Hāpuna Beach Park   Mauna Kea Beach Hotel
Puakō Petroglyphs   Mauna Lani Bay Hotel   Parker Ranch
Hilton Waikoloa Hotel
HĀMĀKUA
'Akaka Falls
State Park
• **Pu'uanahulu**   Observatories
MAUNA KEA   **Onomea**
KONA   *HUALĀLAI*   **HILO**   *HILO BAY*
• **Honokōhau**   Hilo
Ahuena Heiau   **Kailua-Kona**   Rainbow Falls
Hulihe'e Palace
• **Keauhou**   **Kea'au**
KEAUHOU BAY
PUNA
KEALAKEKUA BAY   Hawai'i Volcanoes
Pu'uhonua o Hōnaunau   Volcano House   National Park
Hawai'i Volcano Observatory   Kīlauea Crater
• **Ho'okena**   Kīlauea Caldera   Thurston Lava Tube
Tree Fern Jungle
MAUNA LOA   **Kalapana**
KA'Ū   *Ka'ū Desert*
Chain of Craters Road

Punalu'u
Black Sand Beach

• **Nā'ālehu**

KA LAE
(South Point)